SHA

BEST WISHES HERE!

WICKED SMAHT BABY

A NEW ENGLAND BABY'S BOOK OF FIRSTS

Written & Illustrated by Allison Dugas Behan

To James

ISBN 9781455627325

Printed in Korea
Published by Pelican Publishing
New Orleans, LA
www.pelicanpub.com

WELCOME

NAME

BIRTHDAY

FIRST PICTURE

MY FAMILY TREE

FOOTPRINTS

HANDPRINTS

MY FAMILY

ALL THE DETAILS

TIME

DATE

WEIGHT

HOSPITAL

LENGTH

HOME SWEET HOME

MY FIRST ADDRESS

1 MONTH

MILESTONES & FAVORITES

MONTH PICTURE

2 MONTHS PICTURE

2 MONTHS

MILESTONES & FAVORITES

3
MONTHS

MILESTONES & FAVORITES

4
MONTHS PICTURE

3
MONTHS PICTURE

4 MONTHS

MILESTONES & FAVORITES

5
MONTHS PICTURE

6
MONTHS
MILESTONES & FAVORITES

5 MONTHS
MILESTONES & FAVORITES

6
MONTHS PICTURE

9 MONTHS

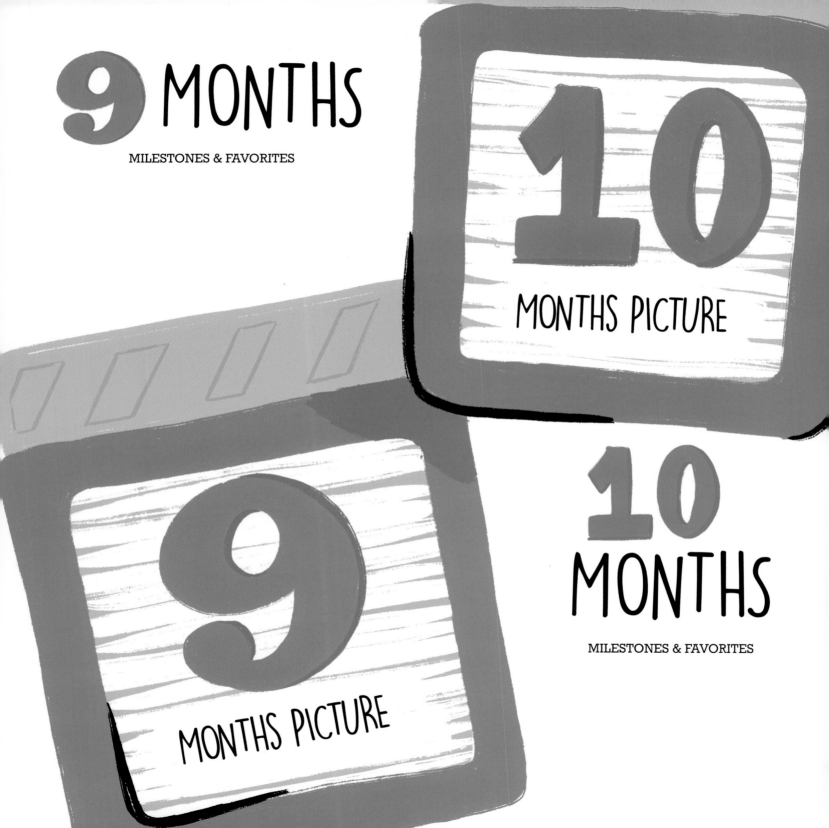

10
MONTHS PICTURE

9
MONTHS PICTURE

10 MONTHS

MILESTONES & FAVORITES

11
MONTHS
MILESTONES & FAVORITES

12
MONTHS PICTURE

11
MONTHS PICTURE

12
MONTHS
MILESTONES & FAVORITES

PARTY THEME

PARTY LOCATION

SPECIAL GUESTS

FAVORITE GIFTS

1

1ST BIRTHDAY

2ND BIRTHDAY

PARTY THEME

SPECIAL GUESTS

PARTY LOCATION

FAVORITE GIFTS

TRYING ALL THE

YUMMY FOOD!

FIRST CLAM BAKE

DATE

WHO MADE IT

MY REACTION

FIRST LOBSTER ROLL

DATE

WHO MADE IT

MY REACTION

FIRST BAKED BEANS

DATE   WHO MADE THEM

MY REACTION

DATE

WHO MADE IT

MY REACTION

FIRST CLAM CHOWDER

FIRST AMERICAN CHOP SUEY

DATE

WHO MADE IT

MY REACTION

FIRST ANADAMA BREAD

DATE

WHO MADE IT

MY REACTION

FIRST MAPLE SYRUP

DATE

BRAND

MY REACTION

FIRST JOHNNYCAKES

DATE   WHO MADE THEM   MY REACTION

FIRST BOSTON CREME PIE

DATE

WHO MADE IT

MY REACTION

FIRST FRAPPE (OR CABINET)

DATE   WHO MADE IT   MY REACTION

FIRST APPLE CIDER DONUTS

DATE   WHO MADE THEM

MY REACTION

FIRST WHOOPIE PIE

DATE   WHO MADE IT

MY REACTION

FIRST ACTIVITIES

AND EVENTS!

FIRST FOOTBALL GAME

DATE

PLACE

TEAMS

FINAL SCORE

FIRST BASKETBALL GAME

DATE

PLACE

TEAMS

FINAL SCORE

GO!

FIRST BASEBALL GAME

DATE

PLACE

TEAMS

FINAL SCORE

FIRST HOCKEY GAME

DATE

PLACE

TEAMS

FINAL SCORE

FIRST LEAF PEEPING TRIP

DATE

PLACE

PEOPLE WITH ME

FIRST
ZOO TRIP

DATE

ZOO NAME

PEOPLE WITH ME

FAVORITE ANIMAL

FIRST
AQUARIUM TRIP

DATE

AQUARIUM NAME

PEOPLE WITH ME

FAVORITE ANIMAL

FIRST MUSEUM

DATE

MUSEUM NAME

FAVORITE EXHIBIT

PEOPLE WITH ME

FIRST VISIT TO BOSTON

DATE

PLACES I EXPLORED

PEOPLE WITH ME

FAVORITE SIGHTS

FIRST BOAT RIDE

DATE

NAME OF BOAT

LOCATION

PEOPLE WITH ME

FIRST TRAIN RIDE

DATE

NAME OF TRAIN

CITIES PASSED THROUGH

PEOPLE WITH ME

FIRST BEACH TRIP

DATE

NAME OF BEACH

FAVORITE ACTIVITY

PEOPLE WITH ME

FIRST STATE PARK

DATE

PARK NAME

FAVORITE SIGHTS

PEOPLE WITH ME

FIRST HOLIDAYS

EASTER

DATE

FAVORITE TREAT

WHERE I CELEBRATED

FAMILY WITH ME

THANKSGIVING

DATE

FAVORITE FOOD

WHERE I CELEBRATED

FAMILY WITH ME

4TH OF JULY

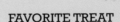

YEAR

FAVORITE TREAT

WHERE I CELEBRATED

FAMILY WITH ME

CHRISTMAS

DATE

FAVORITE GIFT

WHERE I CELEBRATED

FAMILY WITH ME

HALLOWEEN

DATE

FAVORITE TREAT

TRICK-OR-TREAT SPOT

MY COSTUME

NEW YEAR'S

DATE

HOW I CELEBRATED

WHERE I CELEBRATED

FAMILY WITH ME

ALL THE LITTLE EXTRAS

FIRST SMILE

DATE

FIRST LAUGH

DATE

FIRST ROLL OVER

DATE

FIRST CRAWL

DATE

FIRST TIME SITTING UP

DATE

FIRST STEPS

DATE

FIRST TIME I WALKED

DATE

FIRST WORD

DATE

FAVORITE SONG

FAVORITE FOOD

FAVORITE TV SHOW

FAVORITE TOY

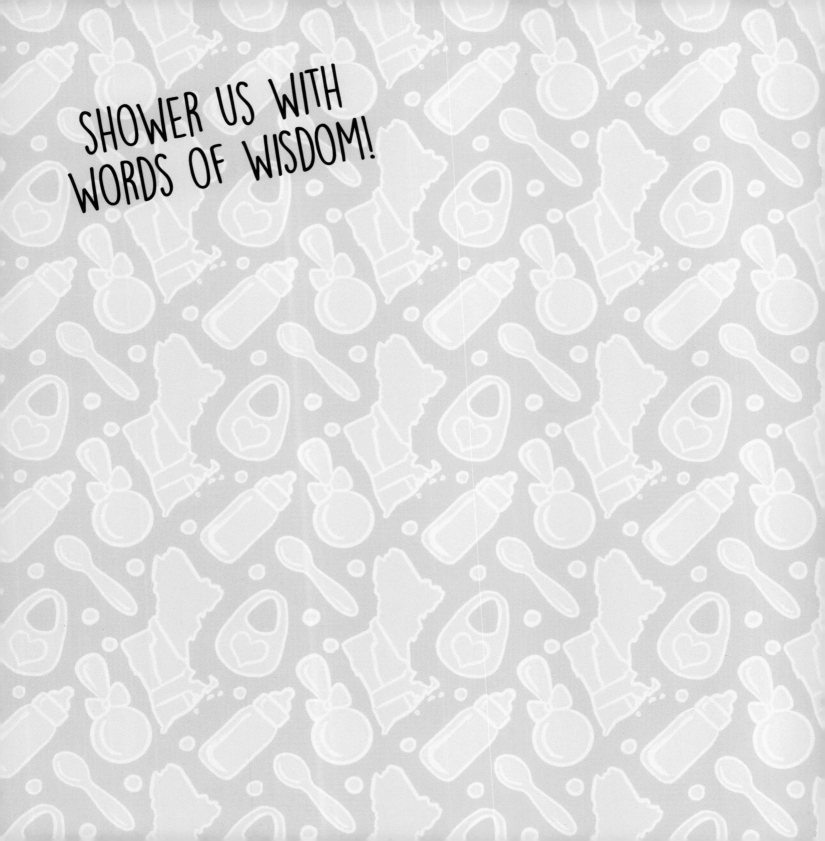

SHOWER US WITH WORDS OF WISDOM!